YOU CAN MAKE IT...

IN HORSE RIDING!

First published in 2002 by Miles Kelly Publishing,
Bardfield Centre, Great Bardfield, Essex CM7 4SL

Printed in Italy

Copyright © Miles Kelly Publishing Ltd 2002

ISBN 1-84236-095-7

24681097531

Series Editor: Paula Borton
Cover Illustration: The Maltings
Layout Design: Mackerel

YOU CAN MAKE IT...
IN HORSE RIDING!

by Victoria Parker

Illustrations   Martin Remphry

Titles in the Series:

Contents

Dedication

In memory of my favourite pony, Polo,
Mum's faithful companion, Mick,
and Liz's mighty steed, George

About the Author

When Vic Parker was growing up, she always wanted to be
the girl in *White Horses* on the telly (ask your mum or dad).
She helped out at her local stables, learned to hack and
jump, and dreamed night and day of having her own pony –
that is, until she got one bruise too many and decided to be
a writer instead. (Well, there's not so far to fall, is there..?)

One Man and his Horse

ABOUT FIVE THOUSAND YEARS AGO
SOMEWHERE ON THE VAST FLAT
GRASSLANDS OF CENTRAL ASIA
AROUND TEA-TIME

...a nomadic tribesman crept out of his tent with a roughly made lasso and stealthily stalked towards a herd of grazing ponies. Every day of his life, the tribesman had watched these beautiful wild creatures gallop across the high plains, and at last he had determined to catch one for himself. Hardly daring to breathe, the bold tribesman drew closer ... and closer ... and closer ... The ponies whickered nervously and flicked their tails. Suddenly the tribesman hurled the lasso – the loop flew threw the air and landed around an astonished pony's neck. The tribesman yelled in delight – for the first time ever, a human had caught a horse!

Alas – the tribesman's joy was short-lived. Less than a second later, the furious pony reared and bolted, leaving the tribesman with severe rope burns on his now empty hands and sprawling on his bottom in the dirt. OUCH. OUCH. And triple OUCH.

Luckily for the whole of humankind, the unfortunate tribesman did not give up. After hundreds more lasso attempts and thousands more bruises, he eventually managed to catch and hang on to his very own pony. And that's how a nameless nomad accomplished one of the most momentous events in human history: the domestication of *Equus* (the proper scientific name for the horse).

Of course, the story doesn't end there. In fact, that's only the very start of it. Next, the nomadic tribesman had to make a paddock to keep his pony in. No doubt the first fence was too low, and the pony jumped it and galloped off – leaving the frustrated tribesman to begin all over again.

The second fence the tribesman built was probably high enough, but too weak. No doubt the pony kicked it down and galloped off again – leaving the sobbing tribesman right back at square one.

When the tribesman finally worked out how to make the right kind of paddock for his pony, he then had to begin the long job of teaching the pony:

– how to obey his commands ...

– how to pull a heavy load ...

– how to carry a heavy load ...

– how to carry the tribesman himself.

And the hard work continued ... Every day the tribesman had to feed his pony, give his pony plenty of water, groom his pony, clear up the pony's poo, and tend to his pony if it was injured or sick. After all that trouble, you can see why he also took precautions to make sure that nobody stole his pony!

Humans have been taking care of horses ever since – and yes, it's still as much effort today as it was then. But the rewards have been huge. For thousands of years, horses have helped us humans to work, hunt, fight, travel and play sports. Humans and horses have become best friends – there are many legendary partnerships. The Roman Emperor Caligula thought so much of his horse, Incitatus, that he gave him a gold water bucket, kept him in a marble stable, and appointed him to the Senate (the Roman government)! When Alexander the Great's courageous stallion Bucephalus died, he founded an entire city in his honour. French Emperor Napoleon called his trusty warhorse Marengo after his greatest battle victory (you can see Marengo's skeleton in the National Army Museum in London). Then there's racehorse Aldaniti and jockey Bob Champion, who was recovering from cancer when they raced together to victory in the 1981 Grand National. And don't forget famous film partnerships like the Lone Ranger and Silver, and Elizabeth Taylor and the Pie in the heart-stopping *National Velvet.*

If you've been bitten by the horse bug (hopefully not stung by the horsefly, as that's exceedingly painful!), this book will tell you all you need to know to make it in horse-riding. Whatever you want to be – whether a top show-jumper, jockey, riding instructor, groom, farrier, teacher of riding for the disabled, riding holiday organiser, mounted police officer, or South American gaucho – you'll need to know the weird and wonderful world of the horse inside out, back to front and upside down ... as well as at a hair-raising gallop. So to find out when a frog is not a frog, when white is actually grey, how being bomb proof can have nothing to do with bombs, and what on earth a numnah is, read on.

Let's Talk Horse...

Do you want the good news or the bad news?

Okay, so let's get the bad news over with first. Obviously, when it comes to making it in horse-riding, the most important thing is to be an excellent rider. This will take years of practice, probably all of your life savings, and a severely bruised bottom on a regular basis.

Fret not. Here comes the good news. You can get a great headstart another way. Okay, so you may not *look* like a horse expert yet, but you can at least *sound* like one. Yes, we're talking horse-speak. And boy, is there a lot of it! The horse world has a whole language of its own – and here's where you can begin to master it. Maybe you know some equine expressions already? Let's find out ...

PONY PUZZLERS

1 What is a coronet?
  a a type of tiara
  b a piece of fisherman's equipment
  c the part of a bridle that goes across a horse's forehead
  d a band around the top of a horse's hoof

2 What is a blaze?
  a a school jacket that you've grown out of and is now too short in the sleeves
  b a stable that's on fire
  c a type of ribbon that can be plaited into a horse's tail for competitions
  d a broad band of white running from a horse's forehead to its nose

3 What is a stocking?

  a a sock-shaped bag (as big as possible) that you leave out for Father Christmas

  b one half of a pair of tights

  c protective padding you can put on a horse's legs for showjumping

  d white on a certain part of a horse's leg

4 What is piebald?

  a a man who has gone bald through eating too many pies

  b a magpie that has lost all its feathers

  c a horse that is frightened of black-and-white things like magpies

  d a horse which is coloured all over in large black-and-white patches

5 What does 'nappy' mean?

  a pants for babies

  b little bobbles that appear on an old woolly jumper

  c short for 'nut-happy' – a pony that behaves well if you bribe it with pony nuts

  d a stubborn pony who won't do what it's told

6 What is a hand?

a the useful thing on the end of your arm

b help from someone else to do something

c a helpful boy or girl who sweeps up at a stableyard

d a unit for measuring the height of a horse

ANSWERS

Mostly a's

You don't seem to know much more about horses than which end bites and which end kicks. Never mind. After reading this book you'll be discussing forelocks and fetlocks with the best of them.

Mostly b's

You probably think that 'getting to know your pony' means finding out its name. Don't reach for your riding hat and jodhpurs until you've read this book, then you'll be able to canter off with confidence.

Mostly c's

Not bad. You're right in thinking that the answers are all to do with horses – but

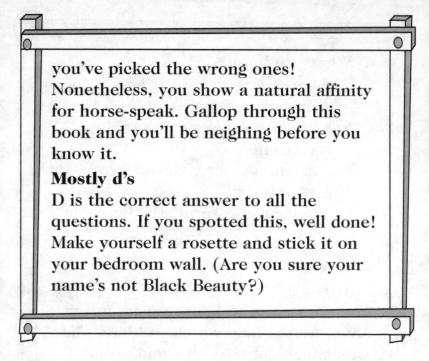

you've picked the wrong ones!
Nonetheless, you show a natural affinity
for horse-speak. Gallop through this
book and you'll be neighing before you
know it.

Mostly d's

D is the correct answer to all the
questions. If you spotted this, well done!
Make yourself a rosette and stick it on
your bedroom wall. (Are you sure your
name's not Black Beauty?)

So if you want to be able to impress the
likes of Frankie Dettori and Lucinda Green
with your perfect pony parlance, here's
what you need to know ...

EQUINE ESSENTIALS

First of all, what's the difference between a
pony and a horse? 'Isn't a pony just a young
horse?' I hear you say. 'Nay!' say I. (Neigh ...
it's a joke – get it?) Ponies and horses are
measured in 'hands'. One hand is four

inches (that's 10 cm to you and me). A pony
is considered to be 14.2 hands or below
(that means 14 hands and two inches, which
is 1.45 m). Anything above this is a horse.
The smallest type of pony in the world is the
Falabella. Falabellas
come from Argentina
and they're under 8.2
hands – that's a
teeny tiny 85 cm!
They're far too small
to be ridden and are
usually just kept as pets.
On the other hand (another horsey pun
there!), the largest type of horse in the
world is the British Shire horse. These can be
over 17 hands – a giant 1.7 m or more – and
may weigh over a tonne, but they're
extremely gentle and kind.

Ready for some more vital vocab? Any
horse under one year old is called a foal. A
young male pony or horse is called a colt –
unless it can no longer breed, in which case

it is called a gelding. An adult male pony or horse that can be used for breeding is called a stallion. An adult female pony or horse is a mare. And yes, you really can tell a horse's approximate age by looking at its teeth, because they change shape as the horse gets older.

On top of all that, you should know that horses and ponies are all divided into types and breeds. Horses are 'typed' by what they're best physically suited to doing – just like humans. Take Venus Williams, for instance. She's tall and strong and accurate – which makes her an unbeatable tennis player, though she'd probably be dreadful at gymnastics. Prince Naseem Hamed is small and quick and aggressive and makes a superb featherweight boxer, but he'd most likely be appalling at the high jump. Similarly, horses are 'typed' as hunters or racehorses or polo-ponies etc.

When it comes to a horse or pony's breed, think of it like their family name. Have you heard of Shetlands, Lippizaners and Appaloosas? Well, they're all breeds.

Oh – and one more thing: a horse with both parents of the same breed is called a pure-bred. And don't mistake a pure-bred for a Thoroughbred. A Thoroughbred is a particular breed that's descended from Arab horses. They're the fastest horses alive – the Marion Joneses and Linford Christies of the horse world.

With me so far? Great. Hold on tight – here's some more. Now you're getting the hang of this horse talk, you're probably not surprised to hear that the parts of a horse (such as the chest, mane, tail etc) aren't called anything as simple as 'parts'. They're called 'points'. And put together, a horse's points make up its overall shape, which is called its 'conformation'. Just as humans can have good or bad posture, horses and ponies can have good or bad conformation.

Horses are proud, elegant, beautiful creatures. So you wouldn't want to embarrass yourself in front of your pony, would you? No, thought not. Well, you can spare yourself many red-faced moments up at the riding stables if you take a little time to get to know the most common points. That way, when the time comes that you're told to trim your pony's feathers, you won't start looking all over for its wings, will you?

PIN THE TAIL ON THE PONY

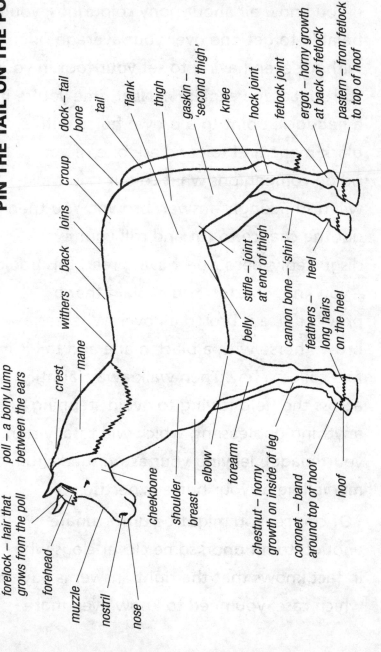

forelock – hair that grows from the poll

poll – a bony lump between the ears

forehead

muzzle

nostril

nose

cheekbone

shoulder

breast

elbow

forearm

chestnut – horny growth on inside of leg

coronet – band around top of hoof

hoof

crest

mane

withers

back

loins

croup

belly

stifle – joint at end of thigh

cannon bone – 'shin'

feathers – long hairs on the heel

dock – tail bone

tail

flank

thigh

gaskin – 'second thigh'

knee

hock joint

fetlock joint

ergot – horny growth at back of fetlock

pastern – from fetlock to top of hoof

heel

A HORSE OF A DIFFERENT COLOUR

If you know all about pony colourings, you'll be able to get one over your average rider without even having to set your foot in your stirrup. Let me explain ... Next time you're in a paddock, point to a brown horse with a black mane and tail and ask one of your riding companions what colour it is. Most will unthinkingly answer 'brown'. You then get the chance to tut and roll your eyes disgustedly, because – having read this book – you know better. You explain that a brown horse is brown all over. Whereas a brown horse with a black mane and tail is in fact called a bay. Then walk away jauntily across the field (trying to avoid stepping in anything unpleasant, which will totally ruin your image), leaving your astonished chum marvelling at your horse expertise.

 Of course, you might be unfortunate enough to hit upon some clever-clogs who in fact knows that the right answer is bay. In which case, you need to know even more horse colours so that you can keep quizzing your irritating friend until you find a horse that they don't know the colour of but you do. So here they all are.

Black	black coat, mane and tail – there might be white markings on the face and legs
Brown	dark brown coat, mane and tail
Bay	brown coat with black mane and tail
Chestnut	light or dark reddish-brown coat, with same coloured mane and tail
Dun	sandy-coloured coat with black mane and tail
Grey	a coat that looks largely white (if it is freckled wth black it is called a flea-bitten grey)

Palomino	gold coat with a white mane and tail
Piebald	large black and white patches all over the coat
Skewbald	large patches of white and any other colour except black all over the coat
Blue roan	black or brown coat mixed with white hairs, and a black mane and tail
Strawberry roan	chestnut coat mixed with white hairs

If your friend is so annoying that they turn out to know *all* the horse colours you ask them, you can still demonstrate your superior knowledge. Ask your friend about face markings instead. There are five main types:

Star	a white mark of any shape on the horse's forehead

Snip	a small white mark on or between the horse's nostrils
Stripe	a narrow white line down the horse's face
Blaze	a broad band of white running from the horse's forehead all the way down to its nose
White face	an even broader band of white than a blaze, which usually includes the forehead, eyes, nose and part of the muzzle

Hopefully by now your friend has been forced to admit that you know much more about horses than they do. If not, you still have an opportunity to wow them. Ask your friend about leg markings. Again, there are five main types:

Stocking	white from the coronet to the knee or hock
Sock	white from the coronet to

	halfway up the cannon bone
Pastern	a white pastern (from the fetlock to the top of the hoof)
Heel	a white heel (the horny bulb at the back of the hoof)
Coronet	a white coronet (the band round the top of the hoof)

If that *still* doesn't do it, hit your friend with the final trick you have left up your sleeve. Ask your friend what a black line all the way along a pony's spine is called. Ha ha – got them!

(By the way, it's a dorsal stripe. Sounds good, doesn't it?)

Starting in the Saddle

So, armed with your new-found knowledge about horses and ponies, you're feeling confident and champing at the bit to get riding. (Or is that your pony?) The first thing to do is to find a top riding school, if you haven't already. Either phone the Association of British Riding Schools in Penzance (on 01736 369440) and ask them to recommend one near you. Or phone the Pony Club at Kenilworth in Warwickshire (on 0247 669 8300) and ask them for the number of your local branch, who should be able to give you the number of a suitable school. Before you commit yourself and your hard-earned cash to lessons, make sure you check out the school in person. When you first start taking lessons you'll just turn up, ride and go home. But as you get more seriously involved in horses you'll want to spend more and more time helping out. So make 100% sure you like your school and the people there, and that they know what they're doing. Here's what you should look for ...

PENNY'S RIDING SCHOOL

CLIPCLOP RIDING SCHOOL

SIGNS OF A STAR SCHOOL

🐎 *A clean and tidy stable yard*

You'll eventually get to know every nook and cranny of the stable yard. This is because the very first way you can show your riding school that you're dead keen on horses is to sweep up ... sweep up again .... and do some more sweeping up.

🐎 *Clean and tidy stables*

Clean and tidy stables not only mean a happy horse, they also mean a happy rider – because eventually you'll be spending a lot of time in here too, and who wants to spend a lot of time in a filthy, stinking cesspit? (No, exactly.) A horse needs to have its stable 'mucked out' thoroughly each day after its breakfast. This means you use a pitchfork to chuck all the pony poo and dirty straw in the stable into a wheelbarrow. (It's not actually as yucky as it sounds, trust me.) You then leave the stable floor to air for a while before you put down new straw for bedding. When you do this, you mustn't forget to 'bank the bedding'. This means building up the bedding along the walls into slopes, to help the horse get up if it lies down. (By the way, 'skipping out' means a quick clean out of droppings only. This needs doing twice a day, before a horse's lunch and tea feeds. Yep, I warned you you'd be spending a lot of time in the stables ...)

A neat and tidy muck heap

The muck heap is where you take your wheelbarrow of mucked-out straw and pony poo. If you stack the muck heap neatly, it helps the dirty bedding to rot down quickly. A neatly stacked muck heap is also the sign of a good riding school because if they can be bothered to take care of their muck heap, they'll certainly take care with their ponies and riding instruction. I should also add that you'll probably be spending a lot of time at the muck heap, as well as in the yard and the stables. This isn't just because of all the mucking out you're going to find yourself doing, it's because if you're as unlucky as me, it's where you'll land whenever you fall off. (Well at least it's nice and soft, eh?)

A clean and tidy tack room

'Tack' is the name for all the bits of equipment your pony wears so you can ride it in comfort. This includes:

- the saddle (The front is called the pommel, the back is called the cantle.)

- the numnah (A special cloth that you can use underneath the saddle.)

- stirrup leathers which attach the stirrup irons to the saddle (You put your feet in the irons when you ride.)

- the girth (The belt which goes under the pony's belly and holds the saddle in place.)

- the bridle (This goes around the horse's head, with the reins attached.)

- the bit (A stainless steel bar which you attach to the bridle and which goes in the horse's mouth. There are lots of different types of bit and the simplest, which you'll probably start with, is called a snaffle.)

If leather tack isn't cared for properly, it can get dry and cracked and will need replacing. A word of warning: leather tack is Expensive (yes, I meant that capital E). Of course, top riders don't want to spend every penny of their Christmas and birthday and pocket money for the rest of their lives on replacing tack. So

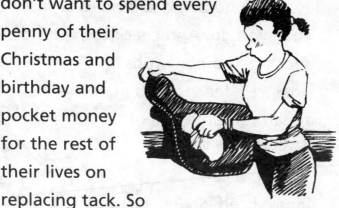

they clean their saddle and bridle with water and saddle soap each time they're used, they oil leather tack from time to time to keep it supple, and they hang it up on racks in the tack room to make sure that other riders and ponies don't tread on it. This means – guess what? – in the end, you'll be spending a lot of time in the tack room, too.

A spacious, well-kept, non-littered paddock

There should be enough grass for all the ponies to graze contentedly when turned out of the stables together. Horses hate being squashed even more than you do. And check the state of the fencing. If a pony rubs up against a fence that's in poor repair (or large bits of rubbish left lying about), it can injure itself. So it's generally safe to say: poor paddock, poor riding school.

🐎 *An indoor arena or outdoor school area (sometimes called a manége), or both*

At last! This is where you'll be having the lessons that are going to turn you into a top-class horse-rider. You might notice strange markers around the sides of the arena, each with a letter on. Now before you get too excited, horses are definitely very intelligent, but no – they can't read. The letters are there for *you*, silly. Once you've learned how to control your pony, your instructor will use the letters to tell you when and in which direction to guide your pony – turning, doing circles and making figures-of-eight. These exercises are called 'school movements'.

HORSEY HUMANS

So far you've learnt all about horses and ponies, and found out what to expect at a good riding school. But what about the *humans* you're going to encounter in the horse world? It's time for you to meet some of the characters at the Martingale Stables & Riding Academy ...

Suzanna Pilkington-Smythe

Mrs Pilkington-Smythe was a top show-jumper in her youth, but a nasty fall put paid to her career in competitions. Now she gets great satisfaction from owning the Martingale Stables & Riding Academy, and instructing and encouraging young riders (although if the truth be told, she likes the ponies more than she likes the children). Mrs Pilkington-Smythe is what used to be described as a 'formidable woman'. She's middle-aged but still looks fantastic in jodhpurs (it's all the riding, you know) and the dads of the academy kids all find her incredibly attractive. The kids, on the other hand, find Mrs Pilkington-Smythe rather less appealing because she has an extremely loud voice which seems to get even louder when she's pointing out their mistakes. When you have a good riding lesson, she always praises your pony. When you have a bad riding lesson, she always blames you! No matter what time of the day or night it is, Mrs Pilkington-Smythe always seems to be at the stables. As she herself puts it: 'I can't go home yet. My husband can look after himself, but my horses need me ...'

♞ *Paula Small*

Paula Small is 19 years old. She's employed full-time as Mrs Pilkington-Smythe's groom and apprentice riding instructor-cum-stable manager. Paula earns pony nuts (the horse world equivalent of peanuts), but she gets free bed and board in a tiny attic room at Mrs Pilkington-Smythe's. Besides, Paula's been riding since she was two and couldn't possibly imagine any other career. A few kids at the riding academy look down on Paula because she always wears the same threadbare sweatshirt, worn-out jodhpurs and mud-caked wellies (she can't afford to buy any new gear). But most of the riding academy kids love Paula. They ask her all the things they're too nervous to ask Mrs Pilkington-Smythe, and they know Paula's always there to help them out with any problems. They also know that Paula's bedroom is covered with rosettes, and they want to be just like her one day.

Arabella Winterbottom

Arabella Winterbottom is one of the kids who sniffs at Paula Small. She has her own pony, Petunia, which her parents pay to have in livery at Mrs Pilkington-Smythe's stables. (That means the pony is kept, fed and groomed by the stable staff.) Arabella has private lessons at the Martingale, where she is dropped off by her daddy in his convertible Mercedes. She always arrives as if dressed up for a show, in a hacking jacket, white shirt and tie, spotless cream breeches and shining knee-high riding boots. Mrs Pilkington-Smythe has tried to explain that for lessons it's only necessary to wear a sweatshirt, comfortable old jodhpurs and ankle-high jodhpur boots – but Arabella just smiles at her reflection in her gleamingly new saddle and adjusts her pristine velvet hard hat. Despite all the money Mr and Mrs Winterbottom are investing in their daughter's horse-riding career, Arabella has yet to master the art of the rising trot.

🐴 *Simon Burke*

Come rain or shine, hurricane or tidal wave, Simon Burke cycles to the Martingale Riding Academy every day at six o'clock in the morning, with the stray dog he rescued snapping at his pedals. Once there, he helps with giving the horses their breakfast, changing their rugs, and mucking out. He cycles back home, changes and goes to school, daydreams about ponies all day in class, and then races back to the Martingale the minute school's finished

to help out again all evening. Simon
Burke is seen sweeping the stable yard
so often that some of the other kids
think the broom is superglued to his
hand. Little do they know that Simon is
passionate about horses, but his family
can't afford to pay for him to have
riding lessons. However,
in return for Simon's
help, Mrs Pilkington-
Smythe makes sure
that he gets a couple
of free riding
lessons a week.
After all, that's
just how she
started off
herself...

 Nigel Chippendale

Nigel Chippendale is the farrier – a
blacksmith who specializes in shoeing
horses. (Fitting horses and ponies with

iron shoes protects their hooves from getting worn down. Don't worry – farriers are specially trained to fit shoes without hurting the animal in any way.) Nigel is a huge bloke about six foot four inches tall, with shoulders wider than Mike Tyson. At least once every six weeks, Nigel turns up at the stables to do his stuff, working up a glistening sweat on his mighty muscles. Nigel loves working with horses – but most of all he likes the long leather chaps he wears over his jeans and being able to flirt outrageously with Suzanna Pilkington-Smythe.

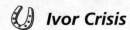 *Ivor Crisis*

Ivor Crisis is the vet that Mrs Pilkington-Smythe calls to the stables if any of her ponies are taken ill. A very intelligent chap, he studied for seven years to qualify as a vet and has since specialized in large animals like horses and cows. He's a man of few words, but Mrs Pilkington-Smythe and her ponies seem to understand him perfectly.

MEET YOUR MOUNT

Great – you now know all about what to expect when it comes to learning to ride. At last, you're ready to get started. All you need now is something to learn on. How exciting! Which of the horses at the Martingale Academy do you think you'll be riding today?

Perhaps it will be the stunning Prancer?

PRANCER

MR SWIFT

Or maybe the haughty Mr Swift?

Or possibly you'd get on best with the beautiful Firefly?

FIREFLY

Wait a minute ... Drum roll, please! Now is the moment you've been yearning for. It's time to meet your pony. Just for you, Mrs Pilkington-Smythe is bringing out — BRYAN.

What's the matter? Surely you didn't expect a firey-eyed stallion with flowing mane and pounding hooves for your first lesson, did you? No, Bryan is the perfect sort of pony to begin on. He's what's known as 'bomb proof' – not frightened of anything. Yep – this is going to be the start of a long and loving relationship between you and Bryan, I can just sense it ...

A Leg up with Lessons

So now you and Bryan have made each other's acquaintance and you're both looking forward eagerly to your first lesson together. This will be fantastically exciting and a bit nerve-wracking at the same time. (If you've already had your first lesson, you'll know what I'm talking about.) Mrs Pilkington-Smythe will teach you how to:

⚘ mount and dismount

Unfortunately, scrambling up at the start of your lesson and then falling off at the end just isn't good enough, I'm afraid. You have to learn to get up and down off Bryan comfortably and stylishly, so Bryan feels comfortable and looks stylish too.

🐎 *sit in the saddle properly*

Good posture in the saddle is called 'having a good seat'. You should keep your head up, your back straight, your elbows in and your heels down. At the same time as you're remembering all this, try to keep relaxed, so you're not like a stiff lump of wood on poor Bryan's back. All this might sound easy enough when Bryan's standing still, but you'll find it's quite a different matter once he starts moving ...

🐎 *adjust the stirrups*

If you were dreaming of being Clint

Eastwood or John Wayne, you'll be disappointed to find that your legs won't be dangling down in the stirrups like cowboys in the movies (unless you're taking Western-style riding lessons, that is). And if you're hankering after riding to victory on the racetrack, you'll be dismayed to see that your feet won't be high up near the saddle like racing jockeys either. Your stirrups will be in between the two.

🐴 hold the reins correctly

Remember that your reins are attached to the bit, which is inside Bryan's mouth. So don't tug roughly on them!

You wouldn't like it if someone was yanking hard on your mouth, and neither will Bryan.

To start off with, Mrs Pilkington-Smythe won't leave you on your own with Bryan but will guide you on a leading rein. Don't worry – this is not because Bryan can't be trusted. In fact Bryan knows exactly what he's got to do – it's *you* who doesn't and who needs help! Mrs Pilkington-Smythe will teach you how to control Bryan by using 'aids' – signals with your arms, legs, bodyweight and voice that tell him to start walking, turn and stop. When Bryan does what you ask, he'll love being rewarded with the occasional pat. But only try patting him when you're confident you can hold the reins in one hand. If you accidentally drop them, Bryan won't be impressed.

SOME IMPORTANT HORSEY DOS AND DON'TS

Mrs Pilkington-Smythe is delighted. You and Bryan have got off to a superb start. But in order for you to remain firm friends with your pony in the future, there are some golden rules that it's never too early to start following:

🐴 *Never* walk behind Bryan. Ponies have a blind spot behind them and if they're taken by surprise, they will kick out. If you're behind Bryan when he kicks out, you won't be behind him for long. You'll be lying in the haystack two fields away, aching all over.

🐴 *Always* check Bryan's girth before you mount. (You should just be able to slide three fingers underneath it.) If the girth isn't tight enough, you'll find that you and your saddle slip round under Bryan's belly quicker than you can say, 'I should have checked the girth'. This is highly embarrassing for both Bryan and yourself.

🐴 It's okay to give Bryan the occasional apple or carrot to say thank you for an enjoyable lesson (as long as you ask Mrs Pilkington-Smythe first, mind you). But make sure that you keep your hand flat and your thumb out to the side when you give him his treat, or you might find that Bryan crunches tastily into your fingers. Needless to say, this does not make for a successful partnership.

HORSING AROUND

Next, to build your confidence and balance on Bryan, Mrs Pilkington-Smythe may get you to do some very strange exercises, such as:

Leaning Forwards

Keeping your legs in the correct position and one hand on the reins, lean forwards and touch Bryan's forelock. (This is one of those occasions when you wish you'd learned the points of a horse, so you know what Bryan's forelock is ...)

Toe Touching

Keeping your legs still, reach down with your right hand to touch your left toes, then do the same on the other side. (Not to be recommended if you've had too many chips for lunch.)

Leaning Backwards

Keeping your feet in the right position,
let go of the reins and lean slowly
backwards until you're lying on Bryan's
back. (You'll probably find this is actually
quite relaxing and pleasant – it's
straightening up again that's a struggle.)

 Round the World

This is where you take both feet out of
the stirrups and swing your legs over
Bryan's back (holding on tightly to the
saddle, of course) until
you've turned all the
way round in a circle
and come back to
where you first started
– with a bit of luck.

You may suspect that these exercises
make you look very silly ... and yes, in
fact they do. But try to forget about
that. Every rider in the world has done
these silly exercises at some time or

other. And every rider in the world has fallen off while doing them too. In fact, there's a saying that goes, 'It takes seven falls to make a rider'. Bear that in mind when you're dusting yourself down and hauling yourself back on (again) ...

TROTTING ON

Just when you feel confident about riding Bryan while he walks, Mrs Pilkington-Smythe announces that it's time to try something a little faster. Now don't get too excited or nervous – she doesn't mean a faster pony. She means going faster on Bryan. Yes, shorten your reins as Bryan lifts his head up higher – you're hot to trot ...

  Now when you see dressage riders in competitions bouncing up and down effortlessly on their dancing steeds, it doesn't give you a hint of the pain that's involved in learning a sitting trot. When you first attempt it, you'll feel like your eyeballs are being bounced out of your head, your teeth being jolted out of your mouth, and you'll lose all feeling in your bottom within the first minute. But stick with it – once you learn to relax and move *with* Bryan instead of just flopping up and down, it becomes a lot less bumpy.

Rising trot is much more fun. This is when you lift your body up and down out of the saddle as Bryan jogs along. Now you feel like you're riding properly for the first time! And if I may say so, you're looking pretty good too ...

FOLLOWING THE HERD

One of the early landmarks in your riding career is the day when Mrs Pilkington-

Smythe decides you and Bryan can be trusted to have a group lesson with other riders. Warning: just because you and Bryan have got on well so far, don't be lulled into thinking that you both now understand each other perfectly. The minute Bryan gets into an arena with other ponies his herding instinct may well kick in. This means that Bryan might refuse to turn and do what you want him to do because he just wants to stick with the other ponies. It might also mean that Bryan hurries too close to the pony in front and earns a swift kick – which gives a new meaning to the saying, 'too close for comfort'.

Not even top riders can read horses' minds, but try to be aware of Bryan all the time, so you can get in quick and stop him from having things all his own way. To help you work out what he's thinking, watch the secret language of ponies' ears. Can you work out which ear position means what?

A – This means that Bryan is listening.
B – This means that you should be prepared for possible trouble – Bryan is cross or scared.
C – This means that Bryan is alert and his attention has been attracted by something.

Answers:

1C   This is generally a good sign that Bryan is interested in the lesson. But remember that it might not always be you that has attracted Bryan's attention. Bryan might just have spotted a particularly luscious patch of grass, which he's about to head straight for ...

2B   Don't panic, this doesn't happen very often. But then again, you find it impossible to be in a good mood 100% of the time and so do ponies. In a worst case scenario, Bryan might suddenly bolt (race off). Keep calm and speak gently to Bryan to calm him down too.

3A   With a bit of luck, it's your instructions he's listening for ...

BYE BYE BRYAN ...

So far so good. After lots of lessons, you're now a competent rider and you're loving it. You might even want to enter some competitions called gymkhanas, just for fun.

Gymkhana events are like obstacle races and party games that you play with your pony. (If you thought your school sports day egg-and-spoon and sack races were tough, imagine trying to do them while leading a pony!) Don't forget that it's not the winning, it's the taking part that counts ... unless of course you win your first rosette, in which case, relish every second of your sweet victory!

However, if you really want to make it in the horse world, you'll have to push yourself on to some more serious stuff. Yes, you'll have to say farewell to faithful old Brian and partner up with ponies who are much more keen on cantering, galloping and jumping.

Riding different ponies will really challenge you and improve your skills. In fact there are some competitions in which riders have to attempt the same showjumping course on each other's animals, to test out who is really the best at getting the most from a horse. But out of all the many wonderful, friendly, agile ponies you'll encounter, you're bound sooner or later to come across the demon pony from hell. Now don't get me wrong, no pony is naughty through and through. I'm talking about a pony that's perfectly agreeable and willing 99.9% of the time – *except on the afternoon when it's your turn to ride it.* The behaviour of the demon pony from hell can take many forms:

- moving off when you're trying to mount
- continually putting its head down to nibble at food
- stopping suddenly and refusing point-blank to walk on

⊍ trying to lie down and roll when you're riding it

⊍ deciding it's had enough of the lesson and trying to bolt out of the arena to get into the paddock.

When this happens to you, do your best not to get angry. Firstly, a pony can sense its rider's mood and your rage will not help to calm him down. More importantly, no rider will ever win a battle of wills or strength with a horse! So you may as well keep your cool. Just continue to ask the demon pony from hell firmly but kindly to do what you want. When it finally obliges, reward it with lots of fuss and maybe a treat or two and it will almost certainly turn back into its usual lovable self in no time at all.

TIPS FOR THE TOP

Here are some top tips for being a first-rate rider ...

🐴 Cantering

Cantering is not just faster than trotting, it's smoother too. The secret of a comfortable canter is to sit well down in the saddle and relax your back, so your hips move with the horse's rocking movement. At first Mrs Pilkington-Smythe might run alongside you, leading your pony on a rein. This is good for two reasons. One – you'll be less nervous and more able to enjoy the speed. And two – you can have a good laugh as she tries to keep up with you and your pony.

🐴 Galloping

This is the fastest a horse or pony can go. To gallop properly, you'll need to have practised the 'forward seat'. This is when you shorten your stirrups by a hole or two and then lean forwards so your bottom lifts up out of the saddle slightly. Make sure you keep your reins short too, so you have control over your pony. Otherwise it might get so excited and carried away that it heads for the hills, carrying you away too!

Jumping

If you've got bags of balance and heaps of confidence, you'll love jumping. You'll start off trotting over poles on the ground before progressing to small, then larger, fences. The correct position for jumping is like the forward seat for galloping. Two essential things to remember are:

1) *don't* pull on the reins to keep your balance, and

2) when you land, allow your pony to stretch its neck out by straightening out your arms.

You'll learn to jump on an experienced pony who will know just what to do. Your biggest problem will probably be if your pony decides at the last minute that he doesn't want to bother to jump after all! If he stops dead and tips you over the top, it is called a refusal. This happens to riders in top competitions like the Olympics on a regular basis. So if you find yourself in the undignified situation of dangling upside down on your horse's head, take comfort from knowing that you're in good company.

JUMPING JARGON

- a *bank* is a type of jump where a horse springs over a fence and a bank on the other side in one leap

- a *bounce fence* is a jump where two fences are so close together that the horse has to land from the first one and take off for the second one straight away

- a *hedge* is a jump with bushy leaves at the top half and a solid part underneath

- a *water jump* is where you jump into, out of, or through water. They're often found in cross-country races.

- if a horse rides around the side of a fence instead of jumping over it, it is called a *run-out*.

A GALLOPING SUCCESS

After you've worked your way through all that little lot you'll be a highly skilled rider. At last you're ready to start making your mark in the horse world by winning some shows. There are lots of events you can try, such as show jumping, dressage and hunter trials. Don't worry if you think you're going to come last, there's another way you can make everyone sit up and take notice of you – make sure that you and your pony are the best-looking creatures there! This means thinking ahead and being well organised. For instance, don't leave it till the night before to discover that the show jumping jacket you last wore six months ago is now too small and won't do up. Or that you'd forgotten all about the huge hole in your best breeches, so you'll have to wear your stained jodhs instead! Prepare your pony well in advance, too. If you give yourself enough time you can wash his mane and tail, and even treat him to a bath if the weather is warm enough. Then you can:

- plait his tail

- plait his mane

- paint oil on to his hooves to make them shiny

- and comb quarter markings on to his hindquarters.

Black Beauty, eat your heart out!

TO FOXHUNT OR NOT TO FOXHUNT, THAT IS THE QUESTION ...

Most people who love horses love all other animals too. So it doesn't make sense why so many riders often take part in chasing a fox over the countryside until it is caught and killed by a pack of hounds ... or does it? Riders who enjoy hunting will argue that it all began in the first place because foxes kill farm animals, so farmers wanted the riders and their horses to do them a favour and get rid of the vermin. Pro-hunting riders will also say that because foxes themselves hunt and kill other animals, why is it so bad when the situation is the other way round? Finally, they'll add that on the vast majority of hunts the fox actually escapes anyway – so nine times out of ten, the riders and horses get an unbeatable and exhilarating cross-country outing with no loss of life at all.

If you *do* decide to ride to hounds, be prepared for certain dangers. And I'm not just talking about the risks of being thrown off into a thorny gorse bush and spending the rest of the weekend pulling prickles out of your bottom. I'm talking about the perils of hunt saboteurs – people who are against fox-hunting and are determined to stop hunts going ahead. If you're lucky, you'll just be accosted by a few angry people in masks shouting things at you like, 'fox murderer' and 'animal killer', and you'll be able to ride off and leave them to it. If you're not lucky, you'll find your photo splashed all across the local press and your school friends sitting across the other side of the dining hall.

At the end of the day, you're perfectly entitled to your own opinion. Nuff said.

GOING THE FINAL FURLONG

So now you can trot, canter, gallop and jump. You've taken part in gymkhanas, moved onto shows and have perhaps hunted too. There's only one thing missing from your picture of perfect happiness – a pony of your own ...

5

Pony Owning

No one has ever wanted their own pony
more than the very first person to make the
enormous effort of catching, taming and
keeping one – our nomadic tribesman. So
nobody is better qualified than he to
hammer home the message that ...

Having your
own pony is
very hard work.

Of course all your efforts will be rewarded by the close, special relationship that will grow between you and your trusty steed – if you don't have a nervous breakdown first because you're so exhausted from looking after it! Read this day from a diary of Tina Trotter, a girl who's lucky enough to have her own pony, and you'll see what I mean ...

FRIDAY OCTOBER 10TH

5.00am

Struggled to wake up – still pitch black outside. Could hear Mum and Dad snoring as usual, snuggled up in their duvet. Managed to creep out of the house without waking anyone. Cycled through the fog to the stables. It's been really damp and cold all this week.

5.30-6.30am

Fed Thumper and changed his water. Looked him all over for a quick health check. Put new rug on him. Mucked out stable and banked his bed. Then led him up the lanes to the field and turned him out. Back to the stables, picked up bike and headed off home. Typical – got a puncture halfway and had to get off and push.

7.00–8.00am

My turn to have breakfast and get washed and changed. Suddenly remembered that I'd forgotten to do last night's history homework as I had to stay late yesterday evening at the stables with the farrier. Panicked. Tried to sit down and do it but realised I'd never have the time.

9.00– 3.30pm

School. Worst nightmare – owned up to Mrs Briton that I'd forgotten homework and she kept me back in detention. Didn't get out of school till 4.15pm. Didn't make it to fetch Thumper until 5pm. Then – cherry on the cake – Thumper wouldn't let me catch him for a good 20 minutes. Never mind, it was worth it in the end as we had a great half an hour's ride together back at the stables. Wish I could have gone straight home, though. Instead, had to groom him, feed and water him, change his rug and skip out. Then still had to clean his tack before I could go home – and didn't even have my bike because of the puncture. Didn't get home till 8 pm. Watched a bit of telly during tea, then had to start tonight's mountain of dreaded homework...

So what do you reckon? Could you keep up this gruelling schedule day in and day out, in all weathers, no matter what else is going on with your family, friends and at school, no matter if you're feeling on top form or a bit poorly? If you have your own pony, he will be totally dependent on you ...

It's not really so different from having a very large, very demanding baby!

Of course, you can always make life slightly easier by placing your pony in livery. This means that you pay to have your pony kept, groomed, fed and generally looked after at a stable yard (like Arabella Winterbottom's pony, Petunia – remember?). This is obviously an ideal situation, since you get all the enjoyment of having your own pony, without the pressure of being responsible for looking after him. But there's a big downside – it's *expensive*. And livery is by no means the only thing you'll have to come up with the cash for if you have your own pony...

EXTORTIONATE EQUINE EXPENSES

● **Grooming kit**

You should try to buy the best quality grooming kit you can – not just because it's better for your pony, but because the equipment will last longer too. Here's the minimum that you'll have to fork out for:

hoof pick – for scraping out mud and stones from the hoof (be gentle around the frog)

plastic curry comb or dandy brush – for getting rid of mud from your pony's coat before you ride it

body brush – for cleaning your pony's coat after you've ridden it

metal curry comb – for cleaning your body brush

sweat scraper – for, well, scraping off your pony's sweat actually!

mane and tail comb – for combing tangles out of the mane and tail

water brush – for making your pony's mane and tail neat and tidy *two sponges* – one to clean your pony's face and another for its dock

stable rubber – to give your pony's coat a final polish

hoof oil and brush – for oiling your pony's hooves

Other assorted equipment

Including tack (which as you already know is Expensive with a capital E) and tack cleaning stuff; stable tools such as a pitchfork, shovel, broom and skip; hay nets, water and feed buckets, rugs. Then there's your own riding clothes, boots and crash hats. Also possibly even the giant-sized expense of your own horsebox, so you can travel with your pony to compete in shows. Oh, and don't forget that your pony will need special protective boots to travel in his horsebox, too.

Feed

Ponies and horses aren't like dogs, they can't survive on just one big meal a day. They have small stomachs (you wouldn't think it to look at them, would you?) and so need three or even four little meals per day, spaced out at regular intervals. The amount your pony needs to eat will depend on how much exercise or work it's doing. As well as providing a big net of hay every day, you'll have to top up your pony's diet with ready-mixed food such as pony nuts and specially prepared cereal mixtures, with some fresh fruit and veg for extra zing! You may also need to put a block of salt called a salt lick in your pony's stable, so it can take in salt to replace the salt it loses when it sweats.

Farrier and veterinary fees

As well as paying for the farrier's regular visits every five or six weeks to shoe your pony, you'll have to stump up the cash for vets' bills now and again. Once a year, you'll have to call the vet to give your pony a vaccination against flu and a disease called tetanus. Twice a year, your vet needs to inspect your pony's teeth. And no matter how carefully you look after your pony, it's bound to get ill or injured sometimes. (Ponies are unpredictable like that.)

A RISKY BUSINESS

I'm sorry to sound like a miserable old nag (spot the awful horsey pun?), but on top of money concerns, pony-owners face two other major worries: 1) poisonous plants and 2) pony stealing.

You'll probably be startled to discover just how many common plants are harmful to horses. Ragwort, bracken, groundsel, buttercups, foxglove, potato tubers, St John's Wort, deadly nightshade and yew can all cause your pony to be horribly ill – at least. Pony owners have to be constantly watchful that their pets aren't about to nibble something that might nobble them.

Then there's the crime of horse theft, which unfortunately is on the rise. Many horse thieves steal ponies the night before a horse auction that's taking place in a different part of the country. By the time the pony's owner has woken up, discovered that their pony is missing and phoned the police, their poor pet has already been taken up the motorway, sold, and is on his way to a new home. Unfortunately, if a thief sets his sights on your pony and is determined to steal it, there's not all that much you can do to stop him. Having your pony freeze-marked might help you identify it later and reclaim it (as might getting a vet to complete a description chart and taking detailed photographs). But the threat of horse theft is a palaver that pony-owners constantly have to live with.

PROCURING A PONY!

So have any of these things put you off wanting your own pony? No, I didn't think they would. You're just as keen as ever, right? Well then, let's see how we're going to get you one. Hmmm – tricky, this ...

At first glance, the way to do it would seem to be to find yourself a paper-round – no, better make that three – sell all your CDs to your mates, negotiate with your parents a fair rate to the do washing-up, make the beds, clean the bathrooms and cut the lawns for ever more ... and in about ten years time you might have enough to buy one leg and the tail.

Not so keen on the sound of that plan? (I wonder why!) Well, you could try any of the following:

* Make friends with the little rich kid at your stables who's got a pony but can never be bothered to ride it or look after it.

* Help out so much at your local stables (for free, of course) that the staff take pity on you and let you ride whenever you like.

* Beg and plead with your parents and generally make their lives so unbearable that they eventually give in and buy one for you. (Nice in theory but highly unlikely in practice.)

Don't be glum! All of the next lot are pony-tastic possibilities:

1 Take up a scheme that many riding schools operate in the holidays whereby you 'own' a pony for a week or so. If that spurs you on (sorry, couldn't resist another dreadful horse pun), then you might then think about ...

2 Leasing or being loaned a pony. This is a situation when the owner of a pony can't take care of it full time for some reason and you agree to either share responsiblity, or even take on the whole responsibility (but on a temporary basis). This is often the perfect way to get your grubby hands on a pony of your own, as you don't have to fork out the thousands of pounds you need to buy one in the first place. But it's essential to draw up a contract in writing so that both the owner and you know exactly who's meant to be doing what when – and also who's meant to be paying for the horse's various expenses. (For instance, are you going to share vets' bills?)

3 If you're not able to lease a pony, then the next best thing is to persuade your parents to let you go on a riding holiday. That way, you at least get to have your own pony for a week (or perhaps longer). Riding out (hacking) across unfamiliar countryside is a thrilling adventure for you and your new companion – just like

something out of horsey storybooks, but even better. (The British Horse Society website has a link to approved riding holiday centres. Check it out at www.bhs.org.uk.)

4   Finally, the British Horse Society have opened a National Rehabilitation Centre at Oxhill in Warwickshire to care for horses and ponies which have been neglected and ill-treated. If you go to their website at www.bhs.org.uk and link into 'Welfare' you'll see that you can choose one of these ponies and adopt it for just £10. Your money will go straight to helping these brave animals, and you'll get a certificate, a badge and a newsletter twice a year to update you on your pony's progress.

Careering Ahead

'Hold your horses!' I hear you cry. 'Where do I go from here?'

Well, you've become a top rider and – whether it's bought, adopted, begged or borrowed – you've even got a pony all of your own. What you need now to finally make it in horse-riding is *a job*. But not just any job. The perfect job. A job that will let you work with ponies and horses for the rest of your life. A job that will pay you good money for doing what you love most in all the world. Sounds appealing? Well, as the saying goes – there are different courses for different horses. So take your pick of whichever of the following careers best suits you ...

HORSERIDING INSTRUCTOR

Are you good at communicating, do you like people as much as ponies, and do you have the patience of a saint? If so, then you're well suited to being a riding instructor. But you'll need to have the right bits of paper. This means passing at least Parts One to Three of the British Horse Society Examinations (you can take Parts One and Two when you're 16, and Part Three when you're 17). You'll also need to pass the BHS Preliminary Teaching Test (you can sit this when you're 17.5 years old) which entitles you to instruct and to run a small yard. The exams consist of both a written paper and practical tests, and cover subjects such as horse anatomy; horse health; knowledge of stable design, saddlery and grassland management; and the ability to give lessons for adults and children. (You can go on and take further qualifications if you wish, such as the BHS Part Four Examination and the Intermediate Teaching Test.)

When you want to work with horses, nothing can beat actual experience. So if you'd like to train 'on the job', the British Horse Society runs Apprenticeships (remember Paula Small at the Martingale Academy?). You can become an apprentice from the age of 16, as long as the BHS agrees and you can find a BHS Approved Yard to take you. You probably won't be paid very much to begin with, but you might be offered free accommodation (and maybe food and laundry too). You'll achieve National Vocational Qualifications and finally the Preliminary Teaching Test.

Qualifying as a riding instructor opens up all sorts of exciting career opportunities. For instance, if you would like to travel and work with horses abroad, you can go on to take the International Trainer's Passport, which is recognised in 27 countries.

On the other hand, you might find that you want to get involved with a riding for the disabled scheme. This can be extremely rewarding and fulfilling. Contact the Riding for the Disabled Association in Coventry for more information. Also, the Fortune Centre of Riding Therapy, Avon Tyrell, Dorset, offers courses in all areas of therapeutic riding.

If you're passionate about the great outdoors, why not channel your instructing skills into running hacking holidays or a trekking centre? You can work towards this from the age of 12, when you're allowed to sit your BHS Riding and Road Safety Test. This will give you the low-down on how to get maximum enjoyment out of riding out while you and your horse stay safe. Later on, you can take British Equestrian Tourism examinations in Riding Holiday Centre Management, Ride Leadership and Assistant Ride Leadership.

JOCKEY

If you yearn for the glamour and excitement of the racetrack, then maybe the life of a jockey is for you. But it's not all applause and champagne, you know. You'll almost certainly have to face fierce competition for a position as a lowly stableboy or girl first. Even though you're an excellent rider, this means going back to doing all the dirty mucking out and tack cleaning jobs while more experienced jockeys get to do all the riding of the Thoroughbreds. You'll also have to be small in height and prepared to keep your weight right down – which means making sacrifices when it comes to most tasty things to eat. But if you're determined and you stick with it, your talent will be spotted in the end. You could one day find yourself asked to ride racehorses for the Queen or the Sultan of Brunei!

Courses for jockeys are run at the British Racing School in Newmarket, Suffolk. You can train here for other exciting careers in horseracing too, such as stable manager and groom.

VET, VETERINARY NURSE, OSTEOPATH, HORSE BREEDER

If you'd rather work alongside horses than ride on top of them, then maybe you should be aiming at being a vet, veterinary nurse, osteopath, or horse breeder.

Bear in mind that you have to be extremely good at your schoolwork to become a vet – particularly in subjects like maths, physics, chemistry and biology. So if you're an academic high-flyer who looks like getting straight A's at GCSE and A level, then go ahead and apply for one of the very few university places that are available for veterinary science. However, if the thought of staying on for A levels and then seven or so further years of university doesn't fill you with deep joy, don't give up. Why not think about becoming a veterinary nurse instead? For more information, contact the British Veterinary Nursing Assocation, based in Harlow, Essex.

Alternatively, if you're good at biology at school and like 'hands on' work, you could train to be an osteopath. Osteopaths are skilled at treating human aches and pains by manipulating bones and muscles into different positions – and some of them specialize in working on animals. Another option perhaps is to go into stud work (horse breeding). The National Pony Society in Alton, Hampshire, offers courses that lead to qualifications in breeding, including a Stud Assistant's Certificate and a Diploma in Pony Mastership.

SADDLER OR FARRIER

Sadly, the skills of saddlery and farriery are dying out and it is often difficult to find craftspeople to take you on and train you. But don't let that put you off!

To be a farrier, as well as being physcially very strong, you need to do an apprenticeship of four years and two months and then pass the Diploma of the

Worshipful
Company of
Farriers (doesn't
that sound
ancient and
grand?). For more
information, contact
The Farrier
Training Service
in Peterborough.

To be a saddler, you can either do a four-year apprenticeship under a Master Saddler, or you can train at Cordwainers College in London or at Walsall College of Arts and Technology in the West Midlands.

PROFESSIONAL RIDER

Don't forget you can aim for jobs with working horses, such as being a mounted police officer or running a company that hires out a horse and carriage for weddings. And if you want to get qualifications to give your business that extra edge, then many colleges and universities are now offering degree courses in horsey subjects, such as a BSc in Equine Sports Coaching. Ask your careers advisor at secondary school for more details.

Last but not least, there's the thrilling life of the professional competitor. Eventing (also known as Horse Trials) is what you see most often on the telly. This sport consists of dressage, cross-country and show-jumping events either held over one day (One Day Eventing) or more demanding competitions held over three days (Three Day Eventing). Dressage looks the least strenuous of the three disciplines but is actually by far the hardest to master. This is where the rider sits so still on her horse that she appears not to move at all, while all the time she encourages her horse to perform complicated footwork and difficult patterns. In contrast, cross-country is like an endurance test for the horse and rider, while show-jumping relies on speed and agility. To become a top competitive horse-rider you'll need to excel in shows and trials at local and then national level. This means creating the perfect partnership between you and your horse.

THE FINAL FURLONG

So that's it. You now know all the inside info on how to make it in horseriding – the ups and downs of a rising trot, the ins and outs of stable life, the highs and lows of soaring over a jump and landing on your bottom in a muddy puddle on the other side.

Don't forget that the path to any dream career is never a smooth ride, so when you come up against a fence across your way, don't just hang up your riding hat and give in. Face it with hard work, courage and determination, then you and your pony will be over the top and galloping off into the sunset together in no time. Good luck!